D0924765

A fan sent in enough four-leaf clover key chains for the whole Blank Page Brigade. Yessss! Now my workplace will be lucky!! Thank you very much.

—*Yūki Tabata, 2015*

YŪKI TABATA

was born in Fukuoka Prefecture and got his big break in the 2011 Shonen Jump Golden Future Cup with his winning entry, *Hungry Joker*. He started the magical fantasy series *Black Clover* in 2015.

3 1901 05735 4377

BLACK CLOVER
VOLUME 4
SHONEN JUMP Manga Edition

Story and Art by YŪKI TABATA

Translation ✹ TAYLOR ENGEL,
HC LANGUAGE SOLUTIONS, INC.

Touch-Up Art & Lettering ✹ ANNALIESE CHRISTMAN

Design ✹ FAWN LAU

Editor ✹ ALEXIS KIRSCH

BLACK CLOVER © 2015 by Yuki Tabata
All rights reserved.
First published in Japan in 2015 by SHUEISHA Inc., Tokyo.
English translation rights arranged by SHUEISHA Inc.

The stories, characters and incidents mentioned in
this publication are entirely fictional.

No portion of this book may be reproduced or
transmitted in any form or by any means without
written permission from the copyright holders.

Printed in the U.S.A.

Published by VIZ Media, LLC
P.O. Box 77010
San Francisco, CA 94107

10 9 8 7 6 5 4 3 2 1
First printing, December 2016

www.shonenjump.com www.viz.com

SHONENJUMP MANGA

WITHDRAWN

Black Clover

YŪKI TABATA

4

THE CRIMSON LION KING

Yuno

Squad: The Golden Dawn
Magic: Wind

Asta's best friend, and a good rival who's been working to become the Wizard King right alongside him since they were little.

Asta

Squad: The Black Bulls
Magic: None (Anti-Magic)

He has no magic, but he's working to become the Wizard King through sheer guts and his well-trained body.

Charmy Pappitson

Squad:
The Black Bulls
Magic: Cotton

She's small, but she eats like a maniac.

Noelle Silva

Squad:
The Black Bulls
Magic: Water

A royal. She's really impudent, but can be kind too.

Fuegoleon Vermillion

Squad: The Crimson Lion Kings
Magic: Flame

A captain with a strong sense of justice. He's Mimosa's cousin and Leopold's

Mimosa Vermillion

Squad:
The Golden Dawn
Magic: Plant

Noelle's cousin. She's calm, gentle and a bit of an airhead.

Nozel Silva

Squad: The Silver Eagles
Magic: Mercury

A proud captain, Noelle's older brother.

Leopold Vermillion

Squad: The Crimson Lion Kings
Magic: Flame

An innocent, self-confident guy. Mimosa's cousin and Fuegoleon's younger brother.

Solid Silva

Squad: The Silver Eagles
Magic: Water

Noelle's older brother.

Nebra Silva

Squad: The Silver Eagles
Magic: Mist

Noelle's older sister.

???

Squad: ?
Magic: ?

A mystery man who's launched a surprise attack on the capital. He has a bitter grudge against the Clover Kingdom…

Sol Marron

Squad: The Blue Rose Knights
Magic: Earth

She's a carefree Amazon, but she adores her captain.

STORY

In a world where magic is everything, Asta and Yuno are both found abandoned on the same day at a church in the remote village of Hage. Both dream of becoming the Wizard King, the highest of all mages, and they spend their days working toward that dream.

The year they turn 15, both receive grimoires, magic books that amplify their bearer's magic. They take the entrance exam for the Magic Knights, nine groups of mages under the direct control of the Wizard King. Yuno, whose magic is strong, joins the Golden Dawn, an elite group, while Asta, who has no magic at all, joins the Black Bulls, a group of misfits. With this, the two finally take their first step toward becoming the Wizard King…

In light of their conquest of the dungeon, Asta and the others are invited to be guests at the distinguished service ceremony, held for Magic Knights who achieve great things. However, they find themselves in a tense standoff with the assembled veterans from each brigade! They then receive word that the royal capital is under attack. Asta and the others leap into action to save the country from peril!

CONTENTS

PAGE 26 ♣ Wild Magic Dance 007

PAGE 27 ♣ We Can Get Stronger 025

PAGE 28 ♣ Blackout 045

PAGE 29 ♣ Bad Loser 063

PAGE 30 ♣ A New Rival 083

PAGE 31 ♣ The Crimson Lion King 103

PAGE 32 ♣ The One Who Waits Deep in the Darkness 123

PAGE 33 ♣ Adversity 143

PAGE 34 ♣ Wounded Beasts 163

✤ Page 26: Wild Magic Dance

WAIT ...
HUH ?!
FSH
!
HUSSSH
GEEZ, KID, YOU CAN MOVE!
I WAS SO SCARED!
Nobody asked...
...for a no-magic nobody like you!!
I GET IT! YOU'RE THAT ANTI-MAGIC GUY!
SCRITCH
AAAAH... AAARRGH ...
QUIT MESSING WITH ME.

KA BO OM
The Capital, Central District
MUR MUR
MUR MUR
OH!!
KA A A A
CITIZENS... STAND BEHIND US.
IT'S THE CAPTAIN HIMSELF! WE'RE SAFE NOW!
THE MAGIC KNIGHTS ARE HERE TO SAVE US!!
IT'S THE SILVER EAGLES !!
MASTER NOZEL!!

West District
I THOUGHT I'D HAVE DESSERT WHEN WE GOT BACK...
...BUT THEIR LOOKS HAVE MADE ME LOSE MY APPETITE.
...
WHAT ARE THESE FIENDS...?! WE CUT THEM DOWN, AND THEY JUST GET RIGHT BACK UP!

YES, THEY ARE. JUST LOOKING AT THEM MAKES ME WANT TO VOMIT.
THESE GUYS ARE SERIOUSLY CREEPY, SIS!
CRIPES!
East District

North-west District
DO THEY HAVE SOME SORT OF WEAK-NESS?
LOOKING FOR IT WOULD TAKE TOO MUCH TIME!
THERE ARE SO MANY OF THEM!

IN THAT CASE...
...BUT THEY'RE NOT LIVING HUMANS!
THESE THINGS... THERE'S MAGIC IN THEM...
North District

WE'LL JUST CRUSH THEM UNTIL THEY CAN'T GET BACK UP!!!

TRY TAKING MY MAGIC!!
Flame Magic: Spiral Flames
KROOSH

Water Creation Magic: Slashing Sea Serpent
SKAA
EYE-SORES !!
SHAA

Earth Creation Magic: Raging Mother Goddess
GRUNCH
QUIT GROSSING MY SISTER OUT!!
Glass Creation Magic: Verre Fleur
SHKKKK
AT LEAST DIE IN ELEGANCE AND BEAUTY!
Oh ho ho ho ho!

Mist Creation Magic: Solid Mist Clones
YOU AREN'T MUCH FUN TO TOY WITH.
SH

Sand Creation Magic: Sand-Armored Heavy Guard
CRUMBLE BEFORE MY MAGIC!!
GRAKKA

Briar Creation Magic: Corpse-Hunting Briar Trees
SWISH
I WILL ALLOW NO ONE TO TOUCH ME!!

BURN TO ASHES !!!
Flame Creation Magic: Leorzenas
NAROOSH

Mercury Magic: Rain Of Silver
ACCEPT YOUR PUNISH-MENT.

PUNISHMENT FOR THE CRIME OF DARING TO THREATEN THE PEOPLE...
...OF THIS COUNTRY.

WHOOOSH
FLAAA
ANYONE WHO'S INJURED, COME TO ME!

THEY'RE FANTAS-TIC!
WHAT AWESOME MAGIC!!
THAT'S THE MAGIC KNIGHTS FOR YOU!!

SLAP
AARRR!!!
DADUM
DUU

WHAT INCREDIBLE STRENGTH!! WHAT A STUPID, RIDICULOUSLY STRAIGHT-FORWARD WAY TO FIGHT!!
I CAN'T BELIEVE IT. HE'S MOWED DOWN THAT MANY WITH HIS SWORD, AND HE JUST KEEPS GOING...

THAT GUY!

HA HA HA HA HA HA!
HEH HEH...

THAT'S EXACTLY WHAT MAKES HIM MY PERFECT RIVAL!!
HE'S JUST WAY TOO INTER-ESTING !!

THAT GUY'S ATTACKS...
THEY INSTANTLY CUT THROUGH THE MANA IN THE CORPSES, ERASING IT!!
MY MAGIC RUNS MY OWN MANA THROUGH CORPSES, MAKING THEM MOVE ANY WAY I WANT.
IT'S WRAITH MAGIC!
WHY?
WHY ARE YOU ATTACKING INNOCENT PEOPLE, YOU SLEAZEBAG?!
GRK
VS
I'M GONNA TAKE YOU DOWN !!

BOOMF!
GRO
NCH
FWOOSH
NUMBER FOUR... JIMMY!
ZZT
...
"Innocent" ...?
BLORP
BLORP

...is a sinner!!
Anyone who doesn't understand my power...

The Assorted Questions Brigade

Good day! Good evening! Good morning!
Here it is, the first question corner.
I'm so relieved we got lots of letters.
Please keep giving us your support!!

Q: Which character do you have the most fun drawing? (Dragon, Tokyo)

A: The one who's most fun to draw is Charmy! She moves around in fun ways. So I guess Asta's fun too.

Q: What's the difference between magic power and mana? (Human with Absolutely No Magic, Kanagawa)

A: Mana is something fundamental and invisible that floats in the air. When mana makes its home in a living creature, it turns into power that can influence other substances, and that's magic power. When magic power is refined even further, it becomes magic... I think that's how it goes. I'm sorry I can't explain it better.

Q: How many members are in the Black Bulls? Also, is the Black Bulls member who says "FSSHHH" TV personality Matsuko Deluxe? (Kouhei Yamada, Fukushima)

A: They've got about a dozen members, I think. Lots of them are free spirits, so I'm not really sure...
The "FSSHHH" person is... There might be a hint in the back of this volume!!

☘ Page 27: We Can Get Stronger

JIMMY JUST GOT YOU WITH HIS SPECIAL-MADE CURSE SHELL. IT'S LOADED UP WITH CURSE POWER!
EVEN SCRATCHES WON'T STOP BLEEDING NOW.
BADMD BADMD
SSK GUK
...
I'M BLEEDING...!
I'd be real careful if I were you!
I WON'T BE ABLE TO SWING THE BIG SWORD FAST ENOUGH!!

RAAAAH!!
BA
BA
BA
BA
BA
BAM

BUT... FIRST...
VUM
VUM
FOR A BRAT WITH NO MAGIC, YOU'RE KIND OF A PAIN...
JIMMY'S STILL GOT LOTS OF CURSE POWER LEFT THOUGH.

HUH ...?

YUMM
Jimmy! Finish off the brat in the back! She's an eyesore!!

BA
SHUF
BA
BA

YOU KNIGHTS PROTECT THE PEOPLE, HUH...
AHH, AHH, THAT'S RIGHT.
SCRITCH
SCRITCH
HA HA HA
WHO'RE YOU AIMING AT?!

VUMMMM
Aim for that brat, Jimmy !!

Ha ha ha ha ha!! Hurry up and abandon her!!
BA BA BA BA
RAAAAH!!
Rrgh ...!
Whoops! No point in getting hurt protecting other people, is there?!
What do you gain out of protecting a little brat like that, you hypocritical loser?!
MISTER!

I'LL PROTECT HER EVEN IF THERE'S NOTHING TO GAIN FROM IT!!

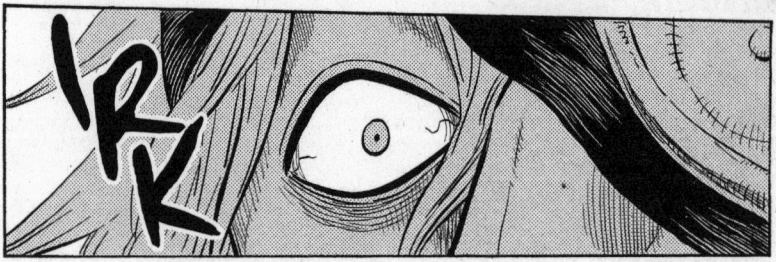
IRK

...and swing your sword around until you bleed to death, moron!!
You will, huh? All right, stay there ...

ASTA!
I HAVE TO HELP HIM, OR ELSE...
HOW... COULD SOMEONE LIKE ME...
...
FLINCH
YOU DO NOT BELONG HERE.
LEAVE THIS PLACE, YOU FAILURE!
GRAW

GADOOM

...

TH...
SHUF
SHUF

THANK Y-

FOCUUUUS!!!
WHUNK!

...
OWWWW

BLACK BULLS GIRL...
DON'T TELL ME YOU'VE LET THE THINGS YOUR SIBLINGS SAID FRIGHTEN YOU.
SHUF
I'M SURPRISED YOU HAD THE NERVE TO RETURN TO THE NOBLE REALM!
YOU WERE FORCIBLY EXILED FROM THE SILVAS!
RIGHT, NOELLE?!
A RECORD-BREAKING EMBARRASSMENT WHO CAN'T EVEN CONTROL HER MAGIC PROPERLY!
...

THERE IS NO TIME FOR SUCH THINGS ON THE BATTLE-FIELD!!
FOOM
AGH
ONE WRONG DECISION MEANS ONE LOST LIFE!!
...

YOU ARE STANDING HERE AS A MEMBER OF THE MAGIC KNIGHTS!
IF YOU JOINED THE KNIGHTS OF YOUR OWN FREE WILL...
...THEN STEEL YOURSELF AND GET STRONGER!!

BEING WEAK IS NOTHING TO BE ASHAMED OF.
STAYING WEAK IS!!
ISN'T THAT WHAT HE KEEPS PROVING...?!
THAT'S RIGHT...

WE CAN BOTH GET STRONGER !!!
HIM ...
ME ...!!
BA
BA
BA
BA
Weak guys die while they're still weak !!
Rrgh ...!!

TWINGE
BADMD
BADMD
WOBBLE
OH N–
BABABA
Water Creation Magic: Sea Dragon's Lair!!
SPLISH
SPLASH
Say what...?!

NOELLE !!

HONESTLY! THAT'S JUST PAINFUL TO WATCH!
I'LL SAVE YOU, SO YOU'D BETTER BE GRATEFUL!!
WHAT ARE YOU DOING, DORKSTA ?!

BAH
You little brats !!

SHUF
HEH HEH HEH
SO YOU'RE BACK IN ACTION, HUH?
IF YOU CAN MOVE FREELY, HE'LL NEVER BE ABLE TO STOP YOU. GO!!

ZUM ZUM

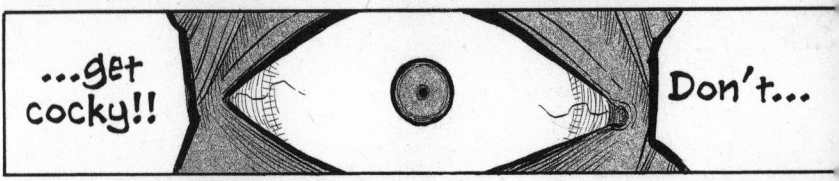
...get cocky!!
Don't...

FWOOSH

GET THAT MONSTER GOOD!!
SHOW ME YOUR POWER!!
BRRR
BRRR
I'LL BACK YOU UP, RIVAL!!
THANK YOU VERY MUUUUCH!!
UMMMMMMM ...
who's that guy?
And...
I WAS GONNA DO THAT ANY-WAY!
GRAAA

WOOM
BA BA BA BA BA BA BA BA
RRRRRR!!!

BA
TUMA
DOOOOOR
CLANG
SPRAAAAT

WHAT AN UN-MAGE-LIKE FIGHTING STYLE!!
YOU'RE WAY TOO MUCH FUN!! BWA HA HA HA HA!!
...
HUH ...?
Don't you dare let a dumb attack like that one take you down...
...Jimmmmm!!!
QUIT GRIPING.
YOU'RE NEXT!
COME AT ME YOUR-SELF!!!
IRK

...and swing your sword around until you bleed to death, moron!!
You will, huh? All right, stay there ...

FOOM
FOOM
WHROOSH
FOOM
FOOM
LET'S HURRY AND EVACUATE!
HEAD CHEF, WHAT ARE YOU DOING?!
Page 28: Blackout
DELIVER THE ULTIMATE DISH UNDER ANY CIRCUMSTANCES!! THAT'S WHAT THE BEST DO!!
YOU FOOLS!! AS IF A CHEF COULD ABANDON HIS COOKING RIGHT IN THE MIDDLE AND RUN!!
BAAAAAM

I'M TELLING YOU, WE NEED TO RUN—
BAH
?!
WELL, IT'S A NATIONAL EMERGENCY, SIR!!
WHAAAAT?! LEAVING WITHOUT EATING MY MAIN COURSE?! WHAT DO THEY THINK THEY'RE DOING?!
YES, BUT THE KNIGHTS ARE ALL GONE! NOBODY'S HERE NOW!
BAAAAAM
LET ME EAT IT, PLEEEEEASE !!!
THAT MAIN COURSE OR WHATEVER IT IS!
SHUFF
AND BESIDES...
THAT'S A MAGIC KNIGHTS ROBE... MEANING... SHE MUST BE ONE OF THE BIG SHOTS WHO GOT INVITED TO THE DECORATION CEREMONY.
CRAFTER
CRAFTER
WHA...? WHO'S THE SHRIMP?
...!

...
SHE'S SOMEBODY SPECIAL!!
SHE'S...
THOSE GLARING EYES OF HERS ARE PRACTICALLY ON FIRE!!
ALL RIGHT, LADY! YOU GOT IT!!
JUST YOU WAIT!! I'LL MAKE YOU THE BEST MAIN COURSE YOU'VE EVER SEEN!!
YESSSSSSSSSS!!!
YAHOOOO
HUH?!
NO, REALLY, LET'S GET OUT OF HERE!!

TH... THAT WAS REALLY GROSS!
PHEW
BADMP BADMP
HMPH... THAT JUST ABOUT DOES IT.
I NEED TO GET STRONGER SO THINGS LIKE THIS DON'T GIVE ME TROUBLE.

NO MATCH FOR US, AT ANY RATE.
...
WHAT WERE THOSE THINGS ANYWAY?

SOL, DON'T SAY THINGS PEOPLE WILL MISINTER-PRET.
I CAN'T BELIEVE YOU TRIED TO ATTACK MY SIS, YOU MORONS!
ONLY THE WOMEN OF THE BLUE ROSE KNIGHTS ARE ALLOWED TO TOUCH HER!

YAAAY
LONG LIVE THE MAGIC KNIGHTS!!
WHAT INCRED-IBLE POWER!!
...
THAT'S ODD.
WHAT WAS THE ENEMY THINKING, UNLEASHING CREATURES THIS WEAK? WHERE IS THEIR MAIN FORCE?
HEH HEH
THAT WASN'T NEARLY FUN ENOUGH.
WA HA HA
WHAT? DONE ALREADY ?!
AAAAA

IT LOOKS AS THOUGH THEY'VE ALL... ENTERED THE MARKED AREAS.
!
GLOW
A FEINT...
BAH
SO WERE THEY REALLY AFTER... THE KING?!

WHAT ...?!
ZUM
ZUM
!!
OH N–
THIS IS...
ZUM
ZUM

Spatial Magic
WELL DONE...
...MAGIC KNIGHTS.
WHA ...
WHAT IS THAT?!

ドドド
Blackout
...

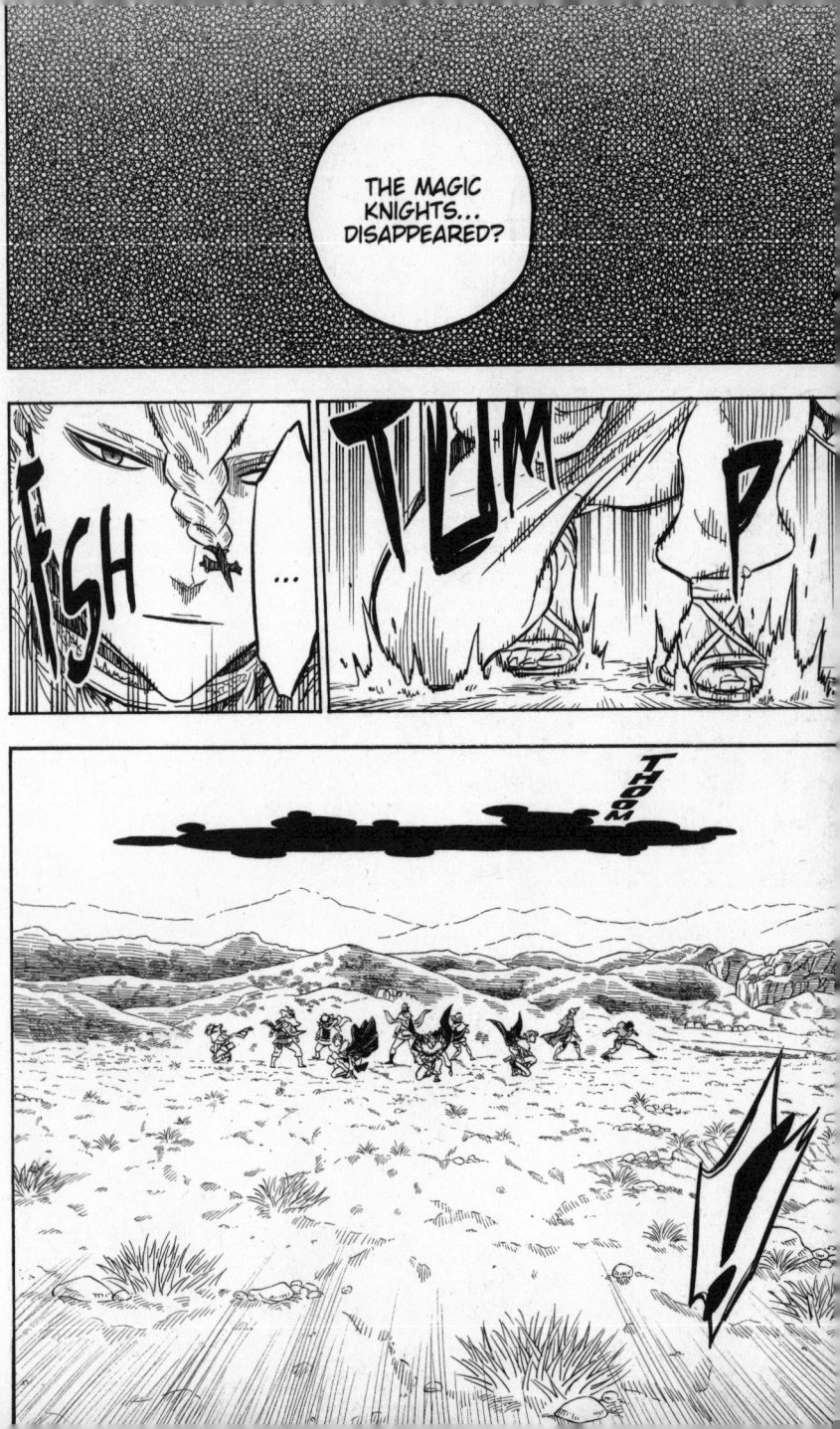
THE MAGIC KNIGHTS... DISAPPEARED?
FSH
...
TUMP
THOOM

I KNEW THE ENEMY HAD A SKILLED SPATIAL-MAGIC USER... BUT I NEVER DREAMED THEY'D BE THIS GOOD!
THEY GOT US!
...
WE SEEM TO BE SEVERAL HUNDRED KILOMETERS AWAY FROM THE CAPITAL, AT THE VERY LEAST.
WHERE ARE WE?!
CURSED!!!
...
ALL THOSE AMAZING MAGIC KNIGHTS FELL FOR A TRAP LIKE THAT ONE?
HOW AMAZINGLY STUPID!

WA
FT
...BUT I GUESS IT WAS POINTLESS.
I WAS PLANNING TO PLAY WITH THE ONES WHO ESCAPED...
MUTTER
WHA...? WHO IS THAT?!
CHATTER
CHATTER
NOW, THEN... WHILE I'VE GOT THE CHANCE...
...WHY DON'T I HELP MYSELF TO SOME NICE YOUNG MANA? ♪

WHOOSH
?!
AAAA

KYA
HA HA
HA HA
AAAAAH!
You sows!!
Quit pretending you're cute!!

MY! YOU'RE KINDA HANDSOME, AREN'T YOU! ♪
AAAAAGH! ELIZA!!

YOU MONSTER!! WHAT HAVE YOU DONE?!

SAY, AM I PRETTY?
HOW OLD DO I LOOK??
COME ON, TELL ME! ♪

Who's a monster ?!
Die !!!
FAA
FUO OM

MY MY MY.
SO SOMEONE DID ESCAPE THAT SPATIAL MAGIC!
WHOOO

OH MY! TALK ABOUT GORGEOUS! ♪ YOU'RE JUST MY TYPE! ♪
Say, listen!
WANNA COME DO SOMETHING FUN WITH ME?
GET AWAY FROM THOSE PEOPLE...
...OLD LADY.
You're dead!!!

FOOM
FOOM

FW IP
FWISSH
WHO ARE YOU CALLING AN OLD LADY?!!
Page 29: Bad Loser

NO
O
N
BOOM
BO
OM
WHROOOSH
THOSE ARE CURSE BULLETS WITH ALL SORTS OF CURSES INSIDE!!
YOU WON'T KNOW WHAT YOU'RE GOING TO GET UNTIL THEY HIT YOU! ♪

WHAT ARE YOU PEOPLE?
WHY DID YOU ATTACK!?
MY, YOU THINK YOU CAN FIGHT AND TALK?
SURE. YOU'RE HANDSOME, SO I'LL TELL YOU. ♪
WE'RE HERE TO ELIMINATE A CERTAIN SOMEONE!! THAT'S WHY!!
!
Well? And?
WHO DO YOU THINK IT IS?
Not that I'm going to tell you!!

WHERE ...
...IS THE WIZARD KING?!

I AM THE RULER OF THIS LAND! IN A CRISIS LIKE THIS ONE, STAYING BY MY SIDE...
...SHOULD BE THE FIRST RESPON-SIBILITY OF THE NATION'S STRONGEST MAGE!
HE'S GOTTEN FULL OF HIMSELF BECAUSE HIS AUTHORITY EQUALS MINE WHEN WE'RE AT WAR, HASN'T HE?!
I AM THE ONE AND ONLY LEADER OF THIS COUNTRY!
REST ASSURED, YOUR MAJESTY. WE, THE ADVISERS OF THE WIZARD KING, WILL PROTECT YOU.
HA HA HA
I'M STEPPING OUT FOR A BIT. IF ANYTHING HAPPENS, HANDLE IT.
ARRRRGH! WHERE DID HE GO, ANYWAY!? HE'S ALWAYS FAR TOO FREE AND EASY ABOUT THESE THINGS!!!

FOOOOOM

...

THE ATTACKS JUST KEEP COMING!
SHE HAS HUGE MAGIC RESERVES!

MY, MY! YOU'RE GETTING CLUMSIER AND CLUMSIER...
WHAT HIT YOU THIS TIME, I WONDER?

BLAM
BLAM

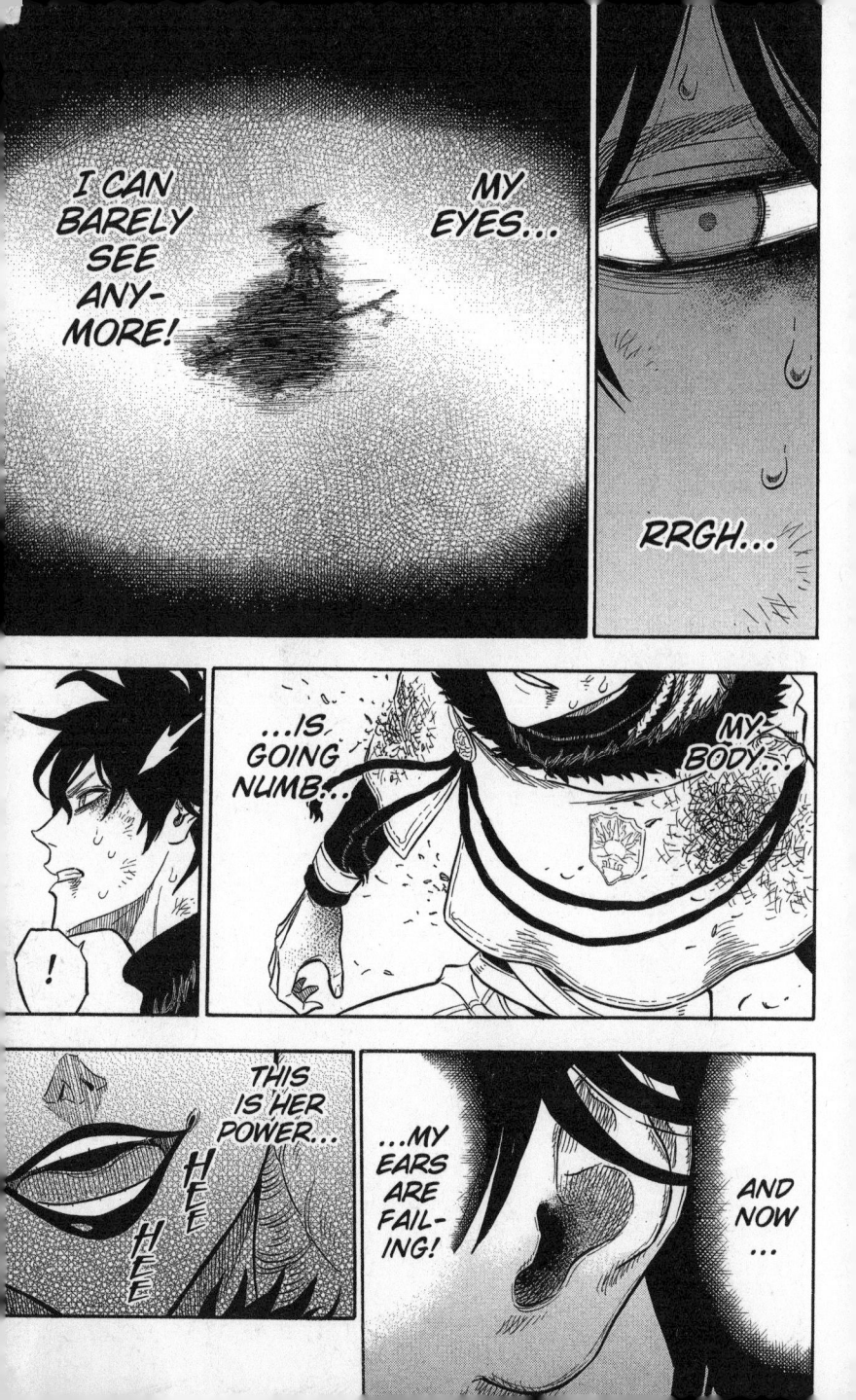
I CAN BARELY SEE ANY-MORE!
MY EYES...
RRGH...
!
...IS GOING NUMB...
MY BODY...
THIS IS HER POWER...
HEE HEE
...MY EARS ARE FAIL-ING!
AND NOW ...

Bit by bit... while trembling with terror...
...you'll pay dearly for calling me old.
ASH CURSE MAGIC, CHEERFUL ASH DESTRUCTION.

...

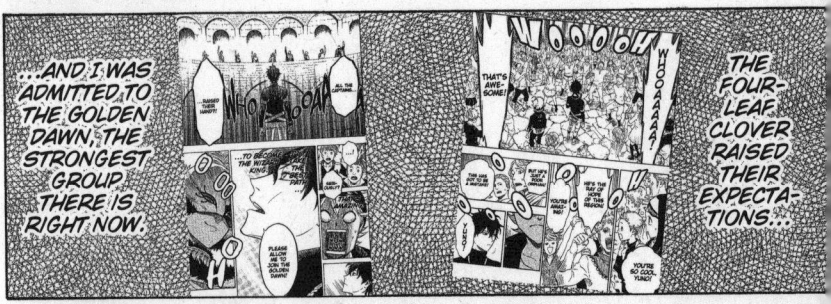
...AND I WAS ADMITTED TO THE GOLDEN DAWN, THE STRONGEST GROUP THERE IS RIGHT NOW.
WHOOOAA
...SAGGY WHITE HAIRS!
ALL THE WAY!
...TO BE THE NEXT KING!
...THE "GOLDEN DAWN"!
WHOOOOOH
THAT'S AWESOME!
WHOOAAAAA!
THE FOUR-LEAF CLOVER RAISED THEIR EXPECTATIONS...
THE KID PUT UP A FIGHT!
THAT'S MY SON, GRANDMA!
YOU'RE THE PRIDE OF THE KINGDOM!
YOUTHFUL PRIDE, YES!
PLEASE ALLOW ME TO JOIN THE GOLDEN DAWN!
YOU'RE SO COOL, YUNO!

...WAS I TRYING TO...
WHAT EXACTLY...

JUST WAIT. HE'LL GO UNDER SOON.
HMPH! HIS ABILITIES ARE NOTHING COMPARED TO THE REST OF THE GOLDEN DAWN.
So maybe he's got a four-leaf clover, but that peasant is pushing his luck.
I WAS ONLY HONING MY SKILLS TO KEEP FROM LOSING.
IT DIDN'T MATTER WHAT OTHER PEOPLE SAID.
...I COULDN'T WIN.
GRIT
GRIT
BUT...
...WAS A POWER I WAS GIVEN BY CHANCE, AND CAN'T CONTROL.
GRIT
GRIT
GRIT
WHAT DEFEATED THAT GUY...

...WON'T LISTEN TO ME AT ALL.
SWING
NOT ONLY THAT, BUT THAT POWER...
BECAUSE THAT POWER, WHICH I REALLY CAN'T CALL MY OWN, REACTED.
IT'S HOW I ESCAPED FROM THAT SPATIAL MAGIC TOO.
GLOW
"...FROM A PEASANT LIKE HIM."
"IT ISN'T AS IF WE'RE EXPECTING MUCH...
...THE THING THAT REALLY FRUSTRATES ME!!
THAT ISN'T...
NO... THAT'S NOT IT.

AND JUST WHAT ARE YOU AIMING AT, HMM?
KYA HA HA HA HA!
HOOM
THOOM
THOOM
You've got to aim properly, like this!!
You know, if you beg for your life very nicely, I don't mind forgiving you!! Say "I'm ever so sorry, miss ♡"!
...
I CAN'T... FEEL AT ALL...
I CAN'T... SEE ANYTHING...
...

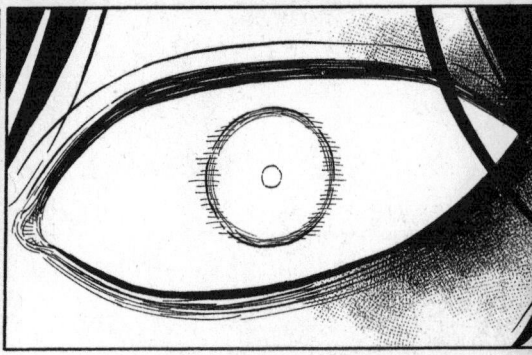

It's said that mages with wind-based mana are particularly good at detecting mana.

...and then attempted to ***go beyond even that.***

...showed an astonishing ability to detect mana...

With all five senses cut off and his back against the wall, Yuno, with his finely honed concentration...

Come on, hurry, tell me!!
I want to know all sorts of things about you! Can you hear me??
KYA HA HA HA
HA HA HA HA
If you don't, I'll kill you right now!!
Go on, go on, hurry up! Hurry and beg for your life!
I DON'T CARE ABOUT YOU.
I JUST...
SHUT UP.
AHH...
HIM...

...TO ASTA!
YUNO'S ...
...TO NOELLE !!!
...MY RIVAL !!!!
SHIING
I DON'T WANT TO LOSE...
I'M NOT DONE YET!!!

HUH?
HUH
!!
THE MANA... IT'S GATHERING ?!
THIS FEELING... THAT BOY...

HE CONTROLLED... MANA?!

THAT GRI-MOIRE !!
THE LEGENDARY...
...FOUR-LEAF CLOVER?!
I'LL TELL YOU...
...JUST ONE THING ABOUT ME.

Wind Spirit Magic:
I'M...
...A REALLY BAD LOSER!!
YEEK!

Sylph's
Breath

✤ Page 30: A New Rival

AAAAAA
YUMMY !!!!
SOOOOOOOOOO...

WHAT ARE THOSE TWO DOING? IT'S A NATIONAL EMERGENCY!
YESSIR !!
GOON
GOON
CHOMP
CHOMP
MUNCH
MUNCH
CHOMP
YOU ARE A PHENOMENAL EATER, SHRIMP!!
GO ON, EAT UP, EAT UP, EAT IT ALL!!

CRASH
!!!

HUH

HUH ...?!
La?
!!

Ooh...
RATTLE
Uggh ...

...
NOT... ENOUGH... MANA!!
YAAH
THIS IS WHY I TOLD YOU WE NEEDED TO RUN!!
A WITCH ...
WE'RE UNDER ATTACK !!

Give it to meee...
Give it to me...
LOOM

I HAVE TO STEAL SOME, OR ELSE ...!
GLEAM GLEAM

ZUM ZUM
Give it to meeee!
NOOOOOOO!

GIVE IT TO HER ...?
MY...MY FOOD?!
NUH...
NOOOOOO!

PPRIN
WHAT IS THAT?!
WAAAAH
!
THE FEEL OF THIS MANA... I KNEW IT! THAT WOMAN'S STILL ALIVE!
THIS GROWING, SWELLING...
Give it to meee!
...MAGIC...

Cotton Creation Magic:
I SAID NO.
HUH?
DOOF
DOOF
DOOF

Strike of the Sleeping Sheep
...

I DON'T CARE WHO THEY ARE— NOBODY TOUCHES MY FOOD!
PHEW
Seriously?!
I WILL FOLLOW YOU MY ENTIRE LIFE, HEAD CHEF!!
HOW D'YA LIKE THAT?! THE PASSION IN MY COOKING POWERED UP THAT SHRIMP'S MAGIC!!
Glad you liked it!!
WHOOOAA
TH... THAT WAS AWE-SOME!!!

SWISH

SWISH
TMPTMP
FOOOOD!!
LAAAAA!

FFT
IN HROOSH
FLOW
OH! A BLACK BULLS ROBE...
Gruuuuub!
THEN IT REALLY WAS HER...!
"GRUB"?
BLURRR
A KID ...?
Gruuub!
THAT TREMENDOUSLY STRONG MAGIC... WAS IT FROM HER?

THERE YOU GO.
I don't know what's going on, but...

?

BADMP

NO PROB.
?
TH... TH...
THANK YOU VERY MUCH!
MY MEAL-SAVING PRINCE HAS ARRIVED!

I'LL HAVE TO...GET BETTER AT USING IT...
TOTTER
I GUESS... THAT SPELL PUTS QUITE A STRAIN ON ME.
LA?!
WOBBLE
UM...UM... C-COULD I ASK YOUR NAME?
!
POOF
FWUP
FLIPPP
LOOK OUT!!
ZZZZ
NOM NOM
W-well... I guess I'd better eat this.
POOF
La... Laaaaa
POOF

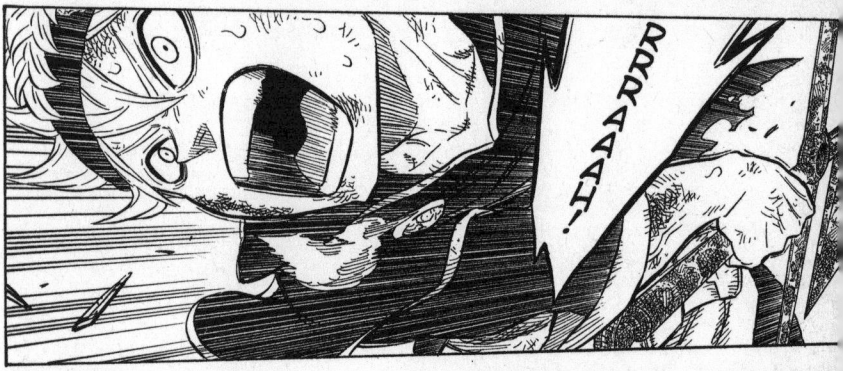
RRRRRRR!

SPAK
SPAK
KRAKZ

KRAKL
KRAKLY
HIRR

Rrgh ...!!

KRAKL
KRAKL
KRAKL
NUMBER TWO... ALFRED.

SPLOOSH

ASTA!!
IF I CAN LEND HIM MY STRENGTH, LIKE BEFORE...

Even that extra-special anti-magic sword of yours ...
...is pretty pointless if your enemy's airborne and you can't touch him.

FWIIISH
BLORP BLORP
BLORP
That guy's your opponent!!
VEUUN
VEUUN
THE WOUNDS THAT GUY GAVE HIM EARLIER ARE...!
BLAAP BLAAP
ASTA!!
...
MUDDY WATER MAGIC!
FOOM
RRGH...
THAT'S A BAD MATCH FOR ME!!

AHAHA
I control corpses and win just by watching! That's how I fight, you moron!!
"Come at me yourself," huh?!
I DON'T WANT TO LOSE TO HIM!!
...
DANG IT...
THIS CRUMMY JERK DOESN'T EVEN THINK OF PEOPLE AS PEOPLE!
MY BODY... WON'T MOVE...
End him, Alfred!!
KRAKL KRAKL
Guts alone ain't gonna get you out of this, kid!!
Hey... What's with that look?!

WHOOSH
SHUT
SHUT
THAT GUY... HE'S...
...JUST LIKE THAT?!
HE TURNED MY ALFRED INTO CHARCOAL...
...!!

MY APOLOGIES FOR HORNING IN ON YOUR FIGHT.
TUMP
I COULDN'T... BEAT HIM...
TOTTER
DANG IT...

I THOUGHT IT WOULD BE A SHAME TO LET A MAN LIKE YOU DIE HERE.
FORGIVE ME!

I HATE TO ADMIT IT, BUT IT LOOKS AS THOUGH YAMI'S FORESIGHT WAS BETTER THAN MINE.

EVEN WITH VERY LITTLE MAGIC POWER, ONE SHOULD BE ABLE TO FLOAT A LITTLE.
WHAT'S GOING ON?
YOU'RE A PEASANT, WITH NO MAGIC.
I'M IMPRESSED YOU FOUGHT THIS FAR.
OKAY, HE'S TOTALLY NOT AMONG THE GUY.
WHY IS HE EVEN HERE?!
WHAT THE HECK, MAN? THAT'S THROW LUMBER-VABLE.

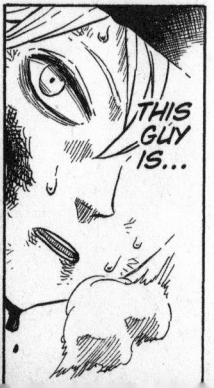
THIS GUY IS...

...YOU AND I ARE RIVALS AS WELL.
SHUF
SHUF
ASTA, WASN'T IT?
YOU SAID YOU WERE GOING TO BECOME THE WIZARD KING.
...TO BECOME WIZARD KING...
...AND SILENCE EVERY LAST ONE OF YOU!!!
Say what?! Become the Wizard King?!
Like a nobody like you could do that!!
IN THAT CASE...

THE CAPTAIN OF THE CRIMSON LION KING MAGIC KNIGHTS...
I GET IT... THIS GUY'S...
FUEGOLEON...
FOOM
LEAVE THE REST TO ME!!
...VERMILLION!!!

Charmy Pappitson

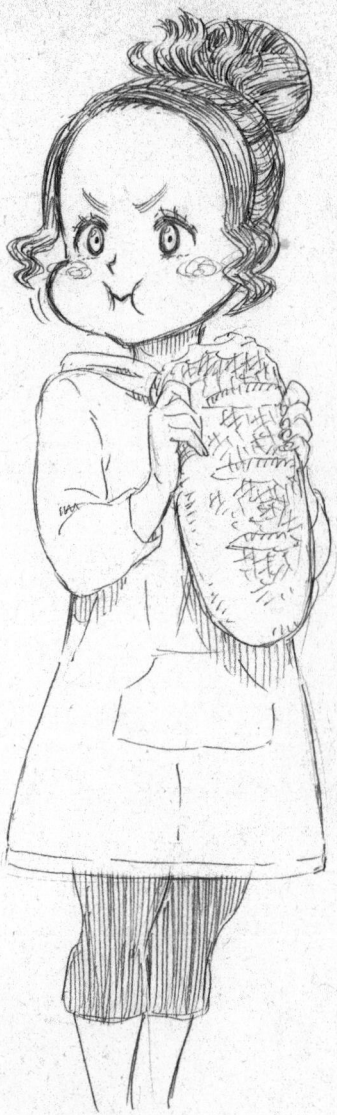

Age: 19
Height: 142 cm
Birthday: June 3
Sign: Gemini
Blood Type: A
Likes: **Food**

Character Profile

Page 31: The Crimson Lion King

"...ARE RIVALS AS WELL."
"THEN YOU AND I...
...JUST CALL ME HIS...?!
DID A MAGIC KNIGHT CAPTAIN...

RRAAAAAAARH!
!
THIS IS NO TIME TO STAND AROUND LIKE A WUSS!!
PAH
I'M STILL GOOD TO GO!!!
NO, YOU'RE NOT.
WUNK
?!

YOUR EXUBERANCE MAY BE YOUR GREATEST WEAPON, BUT KEEP A COOL HEAD AS WELL!
IF YOU REALLY INTEND TO BECOME THE WIZARD KING, THAT IS.
WARRIORS MUST MONITOR THEIR OWN CONDITION, CONSTANTLY DETERMINING WHETHER OR NOT THEY CAN FIGHT.
WOORGH
DRIP DRIP
DRIP DRIP
AT THIS POINT, YOU'RE IN NO SHAPE FOR IT!
WHO ARE YOU?!
YOUR ACTIONS ARE TOO SCATTERED FOR AN INVASION AND TOO ORGANIZED FOR INDISCRIMINATE TERRORISM.
WHAT IS IT THAT YOU PEOPLE WANT?!

...
HAH ...!
SIX YEARS AGO...
...I WAS THE TOP CHOICE FOR A MAGIC KNIGHT SQUAD. THE NAME'S RADES.
...! WHAT ?!
A FORMER MAGIC KNIGHT?!
I WASN'T IMPORTANT ENOUGH FOR YOU PEOPLE TO BOTHER WITH.
YOU DON'T REMEMBER, DO YOU?
...!!
AH...
HE'S A COMMONER, BUT THE STRENGTH OF HIS MAGIC IS PHENOMENAL!

They expelled me!
WITH ALL THAT TALENT, WHY WOULD YOU...?!
THAT MAN...?! AS I RECALL, HE JOINED THE PURPLE ORCAS...
So that's why!! I'm avenging myself against those Magic Knights and the country !!
With this power !!
That's why I'm doing this!!!
ALTHOUGH, YEAH, THERE'S ONE OTHER REASON...!
They said my wraith magic was dangerous, forbidden ...
Since I was a commoner, nobody had my back. They exiled me from both the Knights and the country!!
Wasn't magic supposed to be every-thing?! Huh?!
SKRT SKRT
Better than the nobles... Better than anyone!!
Even though my talents were better...

CHILDISH ...?!
YOU FOOL!! DON'T TOY WITH ME!!
FOR A CHILDISH REASON LIKE THAT, YOU'VE...
They're always simple, y'know?!
That's the thing about reasons.
ZUM
ZUM
BIG BRO...!
LEO !!
...

DO YOU NEED HELP ?!
GLOW
GLUB GLUB
!
THAT'S WHAT I LIKE TO HEAR!!
IF YOU UNDER-STAND WHAT YOU NEED TO DO, THEN GET IT DONE QUICK!!
DEFI-NITELY NOT!!
...
Well, it's not like I'd let you go save him anyway...
HA HA HA HA
Way to ask the impos-sible!!
The affinity between their attributes is lousy!
WH... WHOOOAA... SPARTAN BROTHERS!!
GONG

SORRY, I'M NOT GOING TO BE ABLE TO CONTROL THE INTENSITY OF THIS FLAME.
Flame Creation Magic: Leorzenas
WOOOOOSH

!
KEH HEH HEH
FOOOM

NUMBER ONE, CARL.
WHEN HE WAS ALIVE, THIS GUY WAS A DEFENSE MAGIC EXPERT.
I ADDED MY CURSE MAGIC TO THAT AND MADE HIM EVEN TOUGHER TO GET PAST!!

ASTA.
DO YOU REMEMBER WHAT I SAID A MOMENT AGO?
!

HE'S BRINGING OUT THINGS LIKE THAT AGAIN...!
...

What're you acting all calm for?!
This guy does more than just defend!!

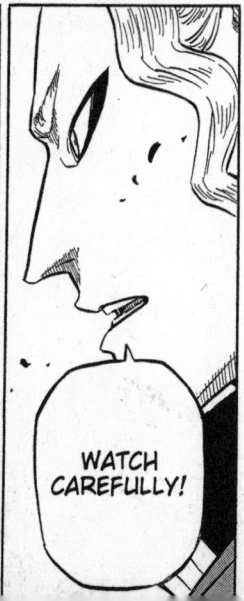
WATCH CAREFULLY!

FLIP
Flame Creation Magic:
Ignis Columna
BOOM
...
Trying to match barrier spells with Carl, huh?!

FWOOOSH
How's this?!
Whaddaya think of this iron defense plus super barrage ?!
I CERTAINLY CAN'T TOUCH YOU...
Ha ha ha ha ha! Is that all you got?!
Mister Captain of the Crimson Lions!!

BOOMF

SPAK

BOOM

...SOL LINEA!
FLAME MAGIC...
!!
I MEET WITH DIFFICULT MAGIC EVERY DAY.
...FOR JUST A MOMENT, THE MANA OF THE BARRIER THINS IN PLACES. I AIMED FOR THAT.
IN THE INSTANT YOU ATTACK ...
LISTEN WELL!!
WHEN IT HAPPENS, IF YOU GAUGE THE ABILITY CALMLY AND MAINTAIN A BOLD FIGHTING SPIRIT, YOU WILL NEVER LOSE!!
BECAUSE YOU ARE MAGIC KNIGHTS, YOU WILL FIND YOURSELVES CONSTANTLY PITTED AGAINST POWERFUL ENEMIES AND MAGIC.

KRAK
KRAK
THAT'S MY BIG BROTHER FOR YOU!!
IS THAT CLEAR ?!
FOOM
YES, SIR!!!
CAN'T BE WASTING TIME ON A GUY LIKE THIS!
FIDGET
SO THAT'S A MAGIC KNIGHTS CAPTAIN!!
FIDGET
MAN... HE'S AWESOME !!!
...
HE SAW THE WEAKNESS IN THAT ONE INSTANT...
...AND HE EVEN PSYCHED UP HIS ALLIES...

RADES, WAS IT?
YOU ...!!
YOU ...!!
NO WAY ...!!
YOU TOOK OUT MY BEST JUST LIKE THAT?!
THERE IS NO ONE WHO WILL ACKNOWL-EDGE...
FLOOM
EVEN IF YOU POSSESS PHENOM-ENAL ABILITIES AND POLISH THEM TO THEIR FULLEST ...
... WITHOUT A JUST SPIRIT, THEY'RE NOTHING BUT VIOLENCE!!
... SOME-THING LIKE THAT!!!
...!!

Fuegoleon Vermillion

Age: 30 Height: 188 cm
Birthday: August 5 Sign: Leo Blood Type: A
Likes: People who want to improve, long soaks in large public baths

Character Profile

☘ Page 32: The One Who Waits Deep in the Darkness

WHY?!
PLANNED FOR TODAY... FOR YEARS! YEARS!!
I RESEARCHED MY OWN MAGIC AS MUCH AS POSSIBLE, HONED IT AND PREPARED!!
I'VE GOT PHENOMENAL POWER, MORE THAN ANYONE!!
AND YET, WHY?!!
BRRR
BRRR
BRRR

RAAAAAH!!
BOOM
SIZZZZZZ
!!
BOOSH
THUD
SPLUT
SPLUT

THAT'S THE SPIRIT! WELL DONE!!
THAT'S WHAT QUALIFIES YOU TO LEAD THIS COUNTRY AS ROYALS!!
WE TOOK ADVANTAGE OF THE GAPS IN THE ENEMY'S MANA AND EVAPORATED IT WITH INTENSE FIREPOWER !!

I got caught up in the moment and actually saluted!
WHIP
YES, SIR!!

I...
AAA
I'VE GOT JUST AS MUCH MAGIC AS A ROYAL!!
IT CAN'T BE...
THAT CAN'T BE...

Leo Palma!!
Flame-Binding Magic:
WHR
OOSH

SHF
BEFORE I DO, I'M GOING TO CONFISCATE YOUR GRIMOIRE.
!

Let me go, you piece of—!!
I'm still...
SHUF
SHUF
THERE ARE MANY, MANY THINGS I WANT TO ASK YOU!
OOO

THIS GRIMOIRE...
SHUF
!
Get your hands off my grimoire!

NOOOOOO!!
TUG
THAT'S IT.

WHAT IS THIS?! THE GRIMOIRE...
IT ONLY HAS ONE PAGE?!
FLIP

THIS GUY... CAN ONLY USE ONE SPELL?!
Give it back !!

Don't you dare ...
... look down on me!!

Don't look!!
Quit looking !!!

Couldn't you have made people acknowledge you some other way?
TOKE
TOKE
!
Who'd look down on you?!
WHAT A WASTE!!
EVEN THOUGH YOU'VE GOT THAT AWESOME MAGIC...
EVEN THOUGH YOU HAVE SO MUCH POWER...
HE
...

SHUF
...WAS A JUST HEART!
YOU WERE ABLE TO OVERCOME ADVERSITY, BUT WHAT YOU LACKED...

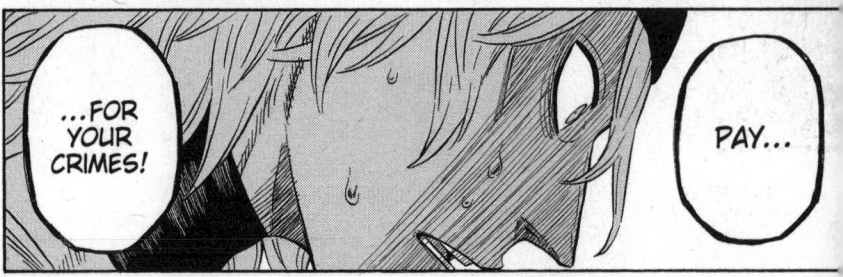
...FOR YOUR CRIMES!
PAY...

GRIT

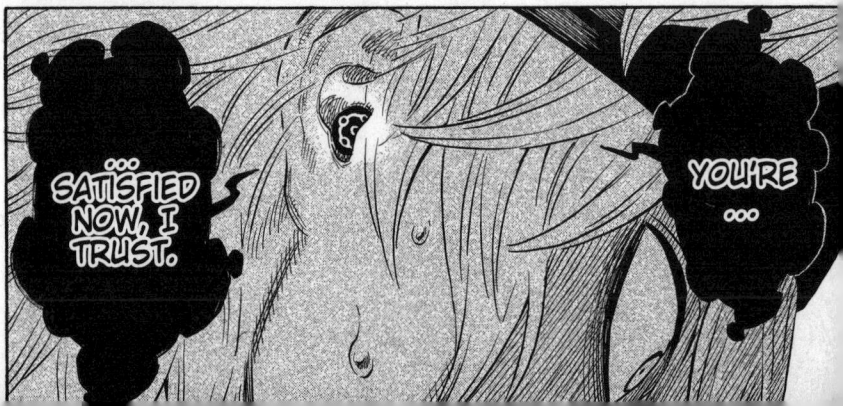
...SATISFIED NOW, I TRUST.
YOU'RE ...

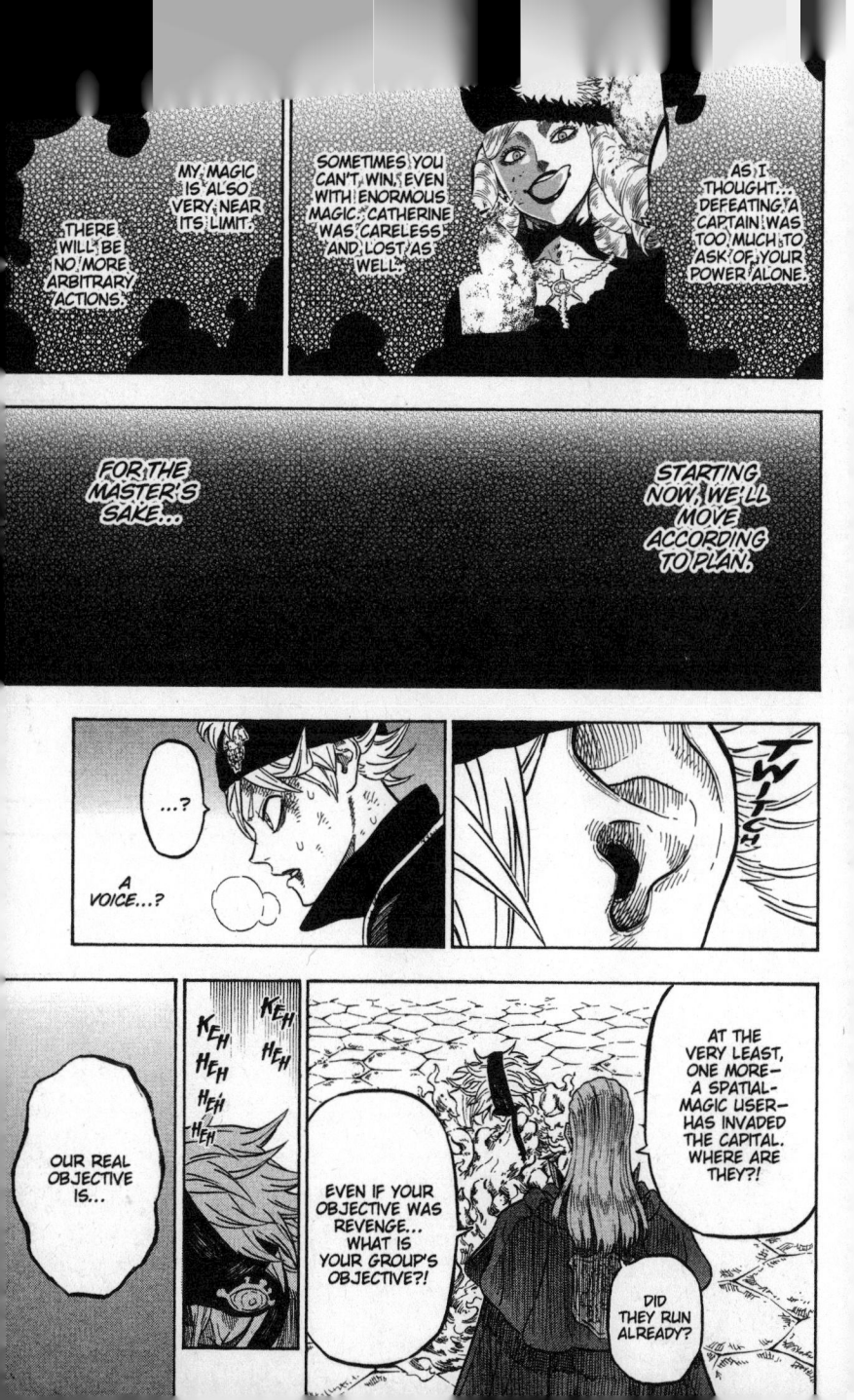
THERE WILL BE NO MORE ARBITRARY ACTIONS.
MY MAGIC IS ALSO VERY NEAR ITS LIMIT.
SOMETIMES YOU CAN'T WIN, EVEN WITH ENORMOUS MAGIC. CATHERINE WAS CARELESS AND LOST AS WELL.
AS I THOUGHT... DEFEATING A CAPTAIN WAS TOO MUCH TO ASK OF YOUR POWER ALONE.
FOR THE MASTER'S SAKE...
STARTING NOW, WE'LL MOVE ACCORDING TO PLAN.
...?
A VOICE...?
TWITCH
OUR REAL OBJECTIVE IS...
KEH HEH HEH HEH HEH
KEH HEH
EVEN IF YOUR OBJECTIVE WAS REVENGE... WHAT IS YOUR GROUP'S OBJECTIVE?!
AT THE VERY LEAST, ONE MORE— A SPATIAL-MAGIC USER— HAS INVADED THE CAPITAL. WHERE ARE THEY?!
DID THEY RUN ALREADY?

YOU!!
FUEGO-LEON VER-MILLION!

WHAT ...?!

!

GRUMBL

THIS IS...!
SPATIAL MAGIC!!
FINE.
NOTHING VENTURED...
BLORP
BIG BROTHER!!!

!
SHUF

AAAAAA
WHAT IS THIS PLACE...?!

!
GRT

YOU'RE ...!

WHERE DID YOU SEND MY BROTHER ?!!
HA HA HA HA HA
YOU FREAK !!!

SO WHERE ...?!
THAT SUPER-ACCURATE SPATIAL MAGIC... THE USER COULD NEVER HAVE DONE IT IF THEY WEREN'T NEARBY!

HA HA HA HA HA
LEO!! THAT MAN ISN'T A SPATIAL-MAGIC USER!
WHAT'S SO FUNNY ?!

HUH?
RIGHT THERE !!!

ZUM
GOOD JOB SEEING THROUGH THAT.
!
...!
HE WAS MIXED IN WITH THEM?!
YOU'RE LIKE A WILD ANIMAL, BOY.
...SO I WENT TO THE TROUBLE OF WEARING THIS FILTHY DISGUISE. AND YET...
I FIGURED IF I DISGUISED MYSELF WITH MAGIC, MAGIC COULD FIND ME OUT...

RIP
BUT...
RIP
...IT APPEARS TO BE OVER NOW.

WHUMP

SZZZZZZZ

FLIE...
...

FLEGLEGLEG

Leopold Vermillion

Age: 16 Height: 164 cm
Birthday: August 13 Sign: Leo Blood Type: O
Likes: Interesting guys, his big brother

Character Profile

Page 33: Adversity
FUEGO LEON!
HE WAS... HE WAS SO STRONG, AND THEY JUST...
IT CAN'T BE...
HJEF
HJEF
TOTTE
THUD
Ghk ...!!
B'DAM B'DAM
HW

FUEGOLEON !!!

FUEGOLEON

THIS CAN'T BE REAL.
MY BROTHER... WOULDN'T LOSE. THERE'S NO WAY...
MY BROTHER... WOULDN'T...
...!!
IF THE GRIMOIRE'S STILL WHOLE, THEN...
RRRIP
THUMP
!
CAPTAIN FUEGOLEON'S...
...GRIMOIRE!!

HE'S STILL ALIVE!!
WE HAVE TO STOP THE BLEEDING !!
IF ONLY MIMOSA WERE HERE ...!!
!!
RATTLE
RATTLE
NO...! THE GRIMOIRE'S STARTING TO CRUMBLE!

LEOPOLD!! HELP ME!
RATTLE
RATTLE
IT CAN'T BE... FUEGO-LEON...
Remember when you mouthed off to me a minute ago?!

OOMF

...
CLATTER
LEOPOLD!!
A MAGIC BLAST?!
A JUST HEART, HUH?!
SHUF
"YOU WERE ABLE TO OVERCOME ADVERSITY. WHAT YOU LACKED...
"...WAS A JUST HEART!"
Go yap your head off in the next world, Fuegoleon Vermillion!!
I always do **just** what my heart tells me to!!

WE'VE DONE WHAT WE CAME TO DO.
LET'S GO, RADES. BEFORE ANY OTHER MAGIC KNIGHTS SHOW UP.
YOUR NAME WAS ASTA, YEAH?
!
STAGGER
HOLD IT... RIGHT THERE!!
Look forward to it, you little punk!!
Well, I'll kill you and make you into one of my toys real soon!!

GRR...
AAAAAAH
THE WAY HE'S BLEEDING, IF HE MOVES AROUND MUCH MORE...
ASTA...! IT'S NO GOOD!
IT'S TOO FAR... I'M NOT GONNA MAKE IT!
...
...TO STOP THAT GUY?!
WHAT CAN I DO...
IT'S JUST LIKE THE CRIMSON CAPTAIN SAID.
CALM DOWN... AND THINK!!
I'M NOT DONE YET!!!
OH!
THAT SPATIAL MAGIC...

NEOWHIS
THIS SWORD IS...
SPAK
WHAT THE...
ANTI-MAGIC !!!

RAAAAAUGH!
ZOOM
Rgh ...!!
THROB
SPLISH
Ah ...!

YAAAAAAGH!!
OWWWWWW!!
Whaddaya think you're doing, trash?!
NOT GOOD.
AFTER YOU HURT ALL THOSE PEOPLE...?
HOW...
...DARE YOU!!
SPEAK

THIS... IS PAIN!!!
YOU LAUGHED AND INFLICTED IT ON PEOPLE WHO HADN'T DONE ANYTHING!!
STOP ...
Especially trash with no magic like you!!!
Getting hurt and bleeding is proof you're weak!!!
People with weak magic should just let people with strong magic kick 'em around.

I'M HERE TO MAKE SURE THAT DOESN'T HAPPEN !!!
AND... I'LL BECOME THE WIZARD KING AND PROVE...
...THAT EVEN PEOPLE WITH NO MAGIC CAN BE THE STRONGEST !!!
...

VALTOS!!
DO SOME-THING!!
IF I COULD, I'D BE DOING IT.
ANTI-MAGIC... IT'S MORE OF A NUISANCE THAN I IMAGINED.
HE'S STORING UP MAGIC...
?!
ZUUUU
FWIIIIN
IT SEEMS WE'LL HAVE TO TAKE CARE OF THE BOY FIRST.
IS HE PLANNING TO ATTACK THROUGH HIS SPATIAL MAGIC?!
!
ZUM

ASTA, LOOK OUT!
TOO LATE.
NO
...

WHAT GOOD DOES IT DO...IF I LOSE MY COOL?!
PHOO
PHOO
STAY CALM AT ALL TIMES. RIGHT, FUEGOLEON?!
HOW PITIFUL.
You little...
SHUF
...
WHAT SHOULD I DO?
WE CAN'T AFFORD TO LOSE RADES YET...

!
!!
HWOOOO
A
...
FIVE OF THEM...!!
REINFORCE-MENTS?!
...PIERCING COLD MAGIC!!
WHAT...

AGAINST PEOPLE LIKE THESE...? PITIFUL.
WE RECEIVED A REPORT FROM OUR MASTER AND CAME, BUT...
ZA
Still... looks like the tables just turned!!
Tch!!
BADMP
BADMP
BECAUSE OF THAT, CURSE POWER, EVEN THOUGH THEY'RE JUST SCRATCHES, THEY WON'T STOP BLEEDING.
IF I LOSE MUCH MORE BLOOD... THINGS COULD GET UGLY.

HEH ...
HEH HEH HEH ...
UWU
ZIP

NOW...
FLAA

!!

WATCH ME, SIR!!
...I CAN KEEP FIGHTING!!

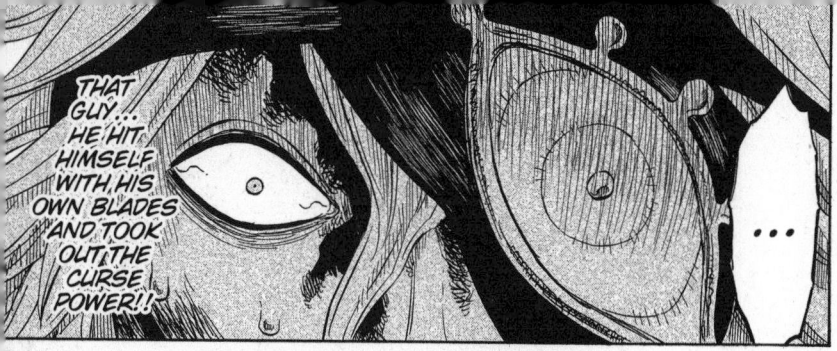
THAT GUY... HE HIT HIMSELF WITH HIS OWN BLADES AND TOOK OUT THE CURSE POWER!!
...

I'VE LIVED WITH ADVERSITY SINCE I WAS BORN.
Y'KNOW WHAT?

...I'LL BLAST THEM ALL AWAY!!!
NO MATTER WHAT HAPPENS OR HOW MANY PEOPLE COME AT ME...

The Blank Page Brigade

This volume's topic:
What lines in the manga made the biggest impression on you?
(A reader submitted this topic!)

♣ Page 34: Wounded Beasts

IT DOESN'T MATTER. HE'S ABOUT TO DIE ANYWAY.
DID THE SIGHT OF OUR NUMBERS DRIVE HIM INSANE?
ROOM
RAAA
RRGH

WHIRR
SPAK
AKAK
!!

YOUR STRUGGLES ARE POINTLESS ...
SPAK
AK

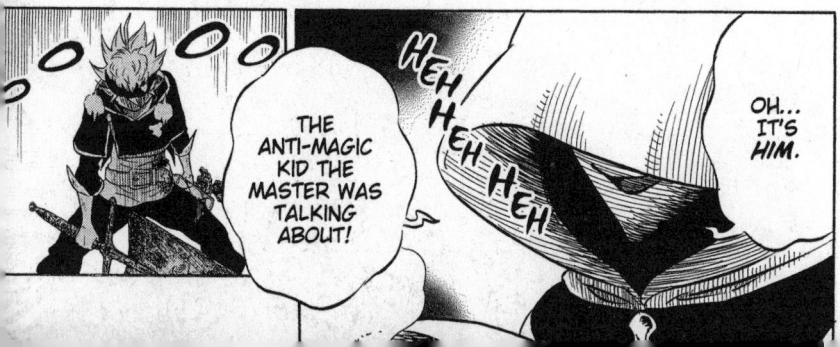
THE ANTI-MAGIC KID THE MASTER WAS TALKING ABOUT!
HEH HEH HEH
OH... IT'S HIM.

YOUR EXUBERANCE MAY BE YOUR GREATEST WEAPON, BUT KEEP A COOL HEAD AS WELL!
HUFF
STAY CALM.
HUFF
RIGHT.
I'M GONNA CALMLY...
...KICK YOUR BUTTS!!
RRAAAAAH!
THAT LITTLE ...!
BOOM!

Flame Magic: Exploding Flames
!!

YOU THINK I'M GOING TO LET YOU PEOPLE THROW YOUR WEIGHT AROUND...
...AFTER WHAT YOU DID TO MY BROTHER?!

LET ME JOIN YOU, MY RIVAL!!
SURE, JUMP RIGHT ON IN!

KAAH!
ARRRG!
TAKE THAT!
THEY SAY BEASTS ARE MORE FORMIDABLE WHEN WOUNDED.
THESE BOYS ARE...

RAAAAR!
...DANGEROUS.

WHOOSH
...WE'LL KILL YOU HERE AND NOW!!

YOU WEREN'T OUR TARGETS, BUT...

Sea Dragon's Lair!!
!!
Water Creation Magic:
SLAP
SLAP
SLAP

WELL, WELL.
SHY
THAT'S QUITE A NICE BARRIER SPELL!

DON'T THINK YOU CAN KILL MY FRIENDS SO EASILY!!

KRAK
KRAK

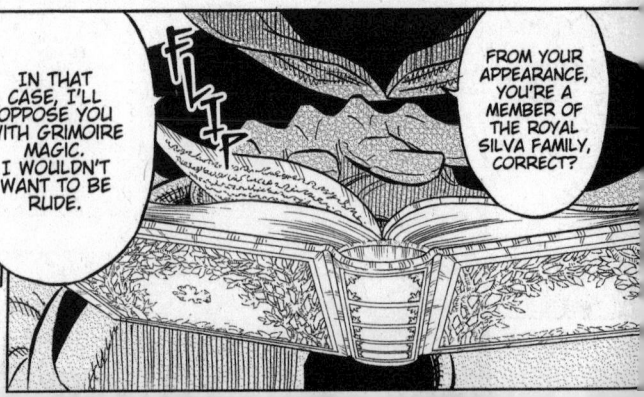
IN THAT CASE, I'LL OPPOSE YOU WITH GRIMOIRE MAGIC. I WOULDN'T WANT TO BE RUDE.
FLIP
FROM YOUR APPEARANCE, YOU'RE A MEMBER OF THE ROYAL SILVA FAMILY, CORRECT?

Tree Creation Magic: Magic-Draining Roots
ZZZT
ZZZT
ZZZT
ZZZT
ZZZT
PLUNK
PLUNK
YOUR FIGHTING INSTINCTS ARE ADMIRABLE.
FLIP FLIP
BA
RAAAAT!
BAH
!!
!!!
SLUURK
SLUURK
NO WAY...!! THEY SWALLOWED THAT TORRENT?!
BLUNK

Wind Creation Magic: Tornado Needles

THOOOOM!!!

STOP!
OOOOOOH
THIS MAGIC... IT'S...!
WHAT ...?
SSSHH
WOOM
SSSHH

MAGIC KNIGHTS!
Y... YOU GUYS...!

IMPOS-SIBLE...!
YOU COVERED THAT DISTANCE THIS QUICKLY?!
HOW DARE YOU SEND US ALL THE WAY OUT THERE?!
!
SHIT

WE REALLY DIDN'T WANT TO...BUT WE ALL WORKED TOGETHER TO GET BACK.
I SUPPOSE I SHOULD CALL IT SUPER COMPOUND MAGIC.

WE REALLY DON'T PLAY WELL WITH OTHERS, YOU KNOW.
TCH!
I'M NEVER COOP-ERATING AGAIN.

HMPH
I'LL ACKNOWL-EDGE THEIR ABILITIES. NO MORE.
WELL, I GUESS MEN AREN'T TOTALLY USELESS.
JOINING FORCES ISN'T BAD, IS IT!
Oh ho ho ho ho!
...

...EXIST TO PROTECT THE PEACE OF THE ONE CLOVER KINGDOM!!
HOWEVER... OUR NINE MAGIC KNIGHT SQUADS...

IT'LL COST US IF WE KEEP FIGHTING. LET'S RETREAT.
TMP
!
TCH...
TMP
Mercury Magic: Rain of Silver
WSSH
WHAT'S THE RUSH?

Gel Magic: Sticky Salamander
GLOORP
FLIP
Dark Magic Item: Special Properties +Alpha... Absorbed!
RMMM

MY RAIN WILL GO RIGHT THROUGH A SPELL LIKE THAT.
AND THEN ...
AB
R
WHAT...
...IS THAT MAGIC ITEM?!
SHUT
BAH
GALOOP
GLUP

WE ARE THE EYE OF THE MIDNIGHT SUN.

ASTA!

BLOOP
WHAT ARE YOU GOING TO DO WITH HIM?
MI—NE!
HEH HEH HEH THAT'S A SECRET. ♪

THEY JUST DEFLECTED A CAPTAIN'S SPELL AS IF IT WAS NOTHING!!
ASTA ...!!
ASTA !!

REMEMBER THIS...
...MAGIC KNIGHTS.
THUD

BLOK
THE ONES WHO WILL DESTROY THE CLOVER KINGDOM!!
ZUM ZUM
ASTAAAAAA !!!
BLOOP
TO BE CONTINUED IN VOLUME 4!

Special project to celebrate the vol. 4 release!!

Special Support Manga from Yuto Tsukuda: "Memories with Tabacchan"

Congrats on the release of *Black Clover* volume 4!! As a reader, I always enjoy the incredible art and composition skills, and the protagonist Asta's straightforward enthusiasm.

Back when I lived in Tabata's neighborhood, we'd meet at the pub night after night and talk about manga for hours on end. Those are terrific memories. Now we both have manga running in the same magazine, and I feel like, "We did it! Go, us!"

Let's both keep giving it our best!!

Food Wars!: Shokugeki no Soma, written by Yuto Tsukuda, currently runs in *Weekly Shonen Jump* and is available as graphic novels!

This volume's topic: What lines in the manga made the biggest impression on you?

"My magic is never giving up!!!" by Asta

Captain Tabata

"So that means... You're a real man, ain't'cha!" by Magna

Comics Editor Tomiyama

"..." by Nero

Editor Zenas !!!

FWOOSH

Editor Katayama

Wife Zenas !!!

"I said *no*." by Charmy

FWOOSH

©

AFTERWORD

This time, Tsukuda Sensei a.k.a., my friend Tsuku-Tsuku, drew a support manga for me! Woohoo! Thank yooooou!!

We're from the same part of the country, and he's close to my age. Since he was a nice person with a good head on his shoulders, I had him hang out with me a lot. Heh heh heh.

He's a really nice guy who gave a flawless speech as the representative of my friends at my wedding.

He's really enthusiastic about manga, and at the pub, although I always said insubstantial stuff, the things he said were really useful, and I always used them as reference. Heh heh heh.

I'm seriously moved that I get to work hard in the same magazine with a guy like that!
"We did it! Go, us!"
Come by the studio to work on roughs again, okay?

Special Bonus Materials

Presenting early sketches of the Silva siblings and more! You can see the process of trial and error they went through before they were completed. By the way, who's the character with a striking resemblance to ***that*** person...??

Noelle Silva

Nozel Silva

Solid Silva

???

Hamon Caseus

Lotus Whomalt

Shiren Tium

Love triangle!
Comedic antics!!
Gang warfare?!

A laugh-out-loud story that features a fake love relationship between two heirs of rival gangs!

Story and Art by
NAOSHI KOMI

NISEKOI
False Love

It's hate at first sight...rather, a knee to the head at first sight when **RAKU ICHIJO** meets **CHITOGE KIRISAKI**! Unfortunately, Raku's gangster father arranges a false love match with their rival's daughter, who just so happens to be Chitoge! Raku's searching for his childhood sweetheart from ten years ago, however, with a pendant around his neck as a memento, but he can't even remember her name or face!

AVAILABLE NOW!

NISEKOI © 2011 by Naoshi Komi/SHUEISHA Inc.

SHONEN JUMP
WWW.SHONENJUMP.COM

RATED T TEEN
ratings.viz.com

viz media
www.viz.com

A KILLER COMEDY FROM *WEEKLY SHONEN JUMP*

ASSASSINATION CLASSROOM

STORY AND ART BY
YUSEI MATSUI

Ever caught yourself screaming, "I could just kill that teacher"? What would it take to justify such antisocial behavior and weeks of detention? Especially if he's the best teacher you've ever had? Giving you an "F" on a quiz? Mispronouncing your name during roll call...*again*? How about blowing up the moon and threatening to do the same to Mother Earth—unless you take him out first?! Plus a reward of a cool 100 million from the Ministry of Defense!

Okay, now that you're committed... How are you going to pull this off? What does your pathetic class of misfits have in their arsenal to combat Teach's alien technology, bizarre powers and...*tentacles*?!

Seraph of the End

VAMPIRE REIGN

STORY BY Takaya Kagami ART BY Yamato Yamamoto
STORYBOARDS BY Daisuke Furuya

Vampires reign—humans revolt!

Yuichiro's dream of killing every vampire is near-impossible, given that vampires are seven times stronger than humans, and the only way to kill them is by mastering Cursed Gear, advanced demon-possessed weaponry. Not to mention that humanity's most elite Vampire Extermination Unit, the Moon Demon Company, wants nothing to do with Yuichiro unless he can prove he's willing to work in a team—which is the last thing he wants!

THE LATEST CHAPTERS SERIALIZED IN WEEKLY SHONEN JUMP

OWARI NO SERAPH © 2012 by Takaya Kagami, Yamato Yamamoto, Daisuke Furuya /SHUEISHA Inc.

www.shonenjump.com www.viz.com

The latest manga from the creator of ***Dragon Ball***

JACO

THE GALACTIC PATROLMAN

Includes a **special chapter** revealing the secret of Goku's origins!

STORY AND ART BY
Akira Toriyama

Retired scientist Omori lives alone on a deserted island while continuing his research into time-travel. His quiet life is interrupted when galactic patrolman Jaco crash-lands and decides to move in with him. This agent from space claims to be elite, but sometimes it can be a little hard to believe. Can Jaco get along with the old man long enough to save the earth from a dangerous threat?

www.viz.com

www.shonenjump.com

JACO THE GALACTIC PATROLMAN © 2013 by BIRD STUDIO/SHUEISHA Inc.

NARUTO

Story and Art by
Masashi Kishimoto

Naruto is determined to become the greatest ninja ever!

Twelve years ago the Village Hidden in the Leaves was attacked by a fearsome threat. A nine-tailed fox spirit claimed the life of the village leader, the Hokage, and many others. Today, the village is at peace and a troublemaking kid named Naruto is struggling to graduate from Ninja Academy. His goal may be to become the next Hokage, but his true destiny will be much more complicated. The adventure begins now!

WORLD'S BEST SELLING MANGA!

NARUTO © 1999 by Masashi Kishimoto/SHUEISHA Inc.

www.shonenjump.com

www.viz.com

BLUE EXORCIST

STORY AND ART BY
KAZUE KATO

THE ORIGINAL MANGA BEHIND THE HIT ANIME!

RAISED BY FATHER FUJIMOTO, A FAMOUS EXORCIST, RIN OKUMURA NEVER KNEW HIS REAL FATHER. ONE DAY A FATEFUL ARGUMENT WITH FATHER FUJIMOTO FORCES RIN TO FACE A TERRIBLE TRUTH – THE BLOOD OF THE DEMON LORD SATAN RUNS IN RIN'S VEINS! RIN SWEARS TO DEFEAT SATAN, BUT DOING THAT MEANS ENTERING THE MYSTERIOUS TRUE CROSS ACADEMY AND BECOMING AN EXORCIST HIMSELF.

Available wherever manga is sold.

www.viz.com

www.shonenjump.com

ratings.viz.com

AO NO EXORCIST © 2009 by Kazue Kato/SHUEISHA Inc.

Stop

YOU'RE READING THE WRONG WAY!

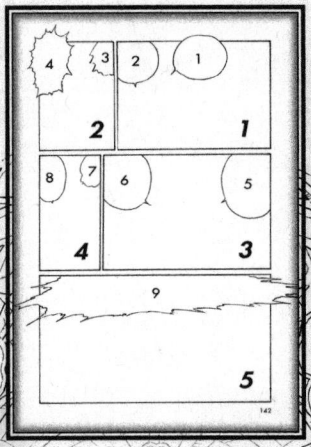

BLACK CLOVER
reads from right to left, starting in the upper-right corner. Japanese is read from right to left, meaning that action, sound effects, and word-balloon order are completely reversed from English order.